FOREVER HIS

A PROMISE OF ETERNAL SECURITY

DR. RON TOBIN

Forever His

A Promise of Eternal Security

DR. RON TOBIN

THE OLD PATHS PUBLICATIONS, GEORGIA

FOREVER HIS

A Promise of Eternal Security

Dr. Ronald Tobin

ISBN: 978-1-7341927-1-1

Print Editions: 2020
Printed in the United States of America
All Scripture is from the King James Version

Tomah Baptist Church
1701 Hollister Avenue
Tomah, WI 54660
608-372-2071
Email: info@tomahbaptistchurch.com
Website: TomahBaptistChurch.com

Published by:
The Old Paths Publications, Inc.
142 Gold Flume Way
Cleveland, GA 30528
www.TheOldPathsPublications.com
TOP@theoldpathspublications.com

TABLE OF CONTENTS

iv

ACKNOWLEDGEMENTS

I would first like to thank all of my pastors and teachers who have trained me. It was they who helped me not only in intellectually understanding eternal security and in intellectually accepting this truth, but emotionally as well. For years I believed that I wasn't perfect or Holy enough for God. For years I was troubled that I wasn't performing enough or that I wasn't up to God's standards or others. I knew I was saved and eternally secure, but I was not able to appreciate the absoluteness of this assurance. Worse still, I wasn't able to enjoy the depths of the love of Christ in and towards me daily. This was true as a young pastor until a pastor, who, I previously worked for in Ft. Lauderdale, Florida came and preached a week of meetings at the church I was pastoring. He excellently and properly expounded I John. What a joy that followed those meetings. Oh, to know and walk in the depths of Christ's great love, no matter my imperfections.

I need to also thank all of those who made this work possible as part of their efforts.

So why a book about "Eternal Security"? Aren't there plenty, one might ask, or is this another Calvinism vs. Armenian book? My answer comes both as a pastor and, hopefully, a balanced Biblicist opposed to both Calvinism and Armenianism extremes.

In fact, both sides in years gone by have referred to the issue as "Assurance of Salvation." For the Calvinist, assurance is reached by rising to a level of spirituality. One then recognizes that you are preserved by the grace, provisions of the Lord's enablement apart from your works. However, your works must prove it. This, of course, is part of their view of predestination and regeneration. For the Armenian, one is also preserved by grace and some human efforts, which one could sin or backslide enough and lose. This then is the evidence of unbelief or fallen grace.

As a pastor, the following can be seen by those who struggle with the concept of eternal security or full assurance. First, there is a level of joy and peace never fully realized. Second, there is the insecure life with a level of constant fear or guilt. It is like a child on a bike being chased by an angry dog. You are always looking over your shoulder to see if some sin, failure, or imperfection is going to catch you. You must keep peddling harder. Finally, there is the unconscious doubt that surfaces. The "am I good enough for God; am I doing enough for God; am I pleasing God enough?" Oh, the emptiness and misunderstanding of His unmovable love which escapes the doubter!

The issue of being Forever Forgiven, Forever Secure, "Forever His" is paramount to *"growing in grace and in the knowledge of Jesus Christ"* 2 Peter 3:18. It is much deeper than accepting a propositional theological truth concerning one's salvation. It is more than being a separated (sanctified) believer. Your personal eternal security is the groundwork for a relationship with Christ, our husband, that is the wellspring of an overflowing abundant life. It becomes the joy of liberation in Christ.

So, let us consider the why and the benefits of being "Forever His".

CHAPTER 1: WHO POSSESSES MY SALVATION

1 Corinthians 6:19-20 *What? know ye not that your body is the temple of the Holy Ghost which is in you, which ye have of God, and ye are not your own? For ye are bought with a price: therefore glorify God in your body, and in your spirit, which are God's.*

The number one question I must ask myself is who possesses my salvation? To put it another way, who owns, controls, or keeps my salvation? Do I keep my salvation? Or is it a co-equal partnership? Or does the Lord keep my salvation? Is Jesus the author (originator) and finisher of my faith?

Hebrews 12:2 *Looking unto Jesus the author and finisher of our faith; who for the joy that was set before him endured the cross, despising the shame, and is set down at the right hand of the throne of God.*

If my saving faith originates and ends with Him, so must all of it in between. If my works can't save or take me to heaven by their merit, then neither can my works of righteousness.

Titus 3:5 *"Not by works of righteousness which we have done, but according to his mercy he saved us, by the washing of regeneration, and renewing of the Holy Ghost;"*

Any moral righteous work I do is either a work of me yielding to the Holy Spirit working in me to will and do

His will, or the pride of the old nature. Salvation is always of the Lord.

Psalms 3:8 *Salvation belongeth unto the LORD: thy blessing is upon thy people. Selah.*

Jonah 2:9 *But I will sacrifice unto thee with the voice of thanksgiving; I will pay that that I have vowed. Salvation is of the LORD.*

Romans 6:14 *For sin shall not have dominion over you: for ye are not under the law, but under grace.*

Romans 8:1-4 *There is therefore now no condemnation to them which are in Christ Jesus, who walk not after the flesh, but after the Spirit. For the law of the Spirit of life in Christ Jesus hath made me free from the law of sin and death. For what the law could not do, in that it was weak through the flesh, God sending his own Son in the likeness of sinful flesh, and for sin, condemned sin in the flesh: That the righteousness of the law might be fulfilled in us, who walk not after the flesh, but after the Spirit.*

Romans 8:9 *But ye are not in the flesh, but in the Spirit, if so be that the Spirit of God dwell in you. Now if any man have not the Spirit of Christ, he is none of his.*

The reason we might think we are partners with Christ in salvation is due to two misunderstandings. The first is due to a low view of our sin nature's corruption. Notice the following Biblical statements.

4

Romans 3:20 *Therefore by the deeds of the law there shall no flesh be justified in his sight: for by the law is the knowledge of sin.*

Romans 7:13 *Was then that which is good made death unto me? God forbid. But sin, that it might appear sin, working death in me by that which is good; that sin by the commandment might become exceeding sinful.*

Romans 7:18 *For I know that in me (that is, in my flesh,) dwelleth no good thing: for to will is present with me; but how to perform that which is good I find not.*

Romans 7:25 *I thank God through Jesus Christ our Lord. So then with the mind I myself serve the law of God; but with the flesh the law of sin.*

Psalms 51:5 *Behold, I was shapen in iniquity; and in sin did my mother conceive me.*

When we get saved, the Lord leaves us with our old sin nature now competing with our new nature of Christ Jesus. What remains is a warfare between the indwelling Holy Spirit's pull and our old sin nature. We must choose who will win, old or new nature.

Romans 7:23 *But I see another law in my members, warring against the law of my mind, and bringing me into captivity to the law of sin which is in my members.*

Galatians 5:17 *For the flesh lusteth against the Spirit, and the Spirit against the flesh: and these are contrary the one to the other: so that ye cannot do the things that ye would.*

The second misunderstanding comes from others malapropping scriptures. Here are a few illustrations:

Philippians 2:12 *Wherefore, my beloved, as ye have always obeyed, not as in my presence only, but now much more in my absence, work out your own salvation with fear and trembling.*

A short-sighted view thinks Scripture is saying that we are the ones responsible to do the necessary works to stay saved. Nothing could be further from the truth. What Paul is telling the Philippians is to practice or perform the salvation you have received ("katergadzomahee") or show that you are fit for it. In both reference are (fear) and trembling. Another passage is found in Hebrews.

Hebrews 6:4-6 *For it is impossible for those who were once enlightened, and have tasted of the heavenly gift, and were made partakers of the Holy Ghost, And have tasted the good word of God, and the powers of the world to come, If they shall fall away, to renew them again unto repentance; seeing they crucify to themselves the Son of God afresh, and put him to an open shame.*

This passage is a little difficult, particularly when we forget that it is written to the "dull of hearing" Hebrew / Jewish professed Christian.

Hebrews 5:12 *For when for the time ye ought to be teachers, ye have need that one teach you again which be the first principles of the oracles of God; and are become such as have need of milk, and not of strong meat.*

They were unable to move on to meat but still were like babies, struggling to return to milk. Therefore (Hebrews 6) the professed believer was being rebuked to move forward and stop going back to foundations of repentance, faith, first doctrines, baptism, resurrection, holiness and last things. They should have graduated from beginner Christianity.

Finally, in verses 4-6, the author reminds the believer that those professing Christ, whose minds were illuminated / enlightened through instruction by the Gospel and the Holy Spirit of their potential dangers. They are on the brink of apostasy, as they had been exposed to the truth but not "partakers". They were not renewed by the Holy Spirit, the heavenly gift.

Plainly he is speaking about false professors not possessors. It is not falling into sin or temptation. The one who falls away (parapipto) is one who intentionally falls away, an apostate. They will never be restored to, or by, a second profession of faith and repentance. They are hardened.

So, our salvation didn't originate with us, nor can we keep it, nor are we expected to.

1 Peter 1:5 *Who are kept by the power of God through faith unto salvation ready to be revealed in the last time.*

It would be prideful to think Jesus only paid a partial penalty for the debt of sin and the rest is up to me. It would make my work equal to His.

7

Jesus, the omniscient God, knows everything about me. He knows my heart, my weakness, my failures, my thoughts, my sins. He knew all this before creation, including my birth, my salvation and my death. Still He loves me and keeps me by His power (1 Peter 1:5)

Praise God! I am "Forever His".

CHAPTER 2: SALVATION IS A LEGAL TRANSACTION

The second reason why we are "Forever His" is because salvation is a legal transaction. It is not based upon a point system, emotions or experiences from day to day. Let us consider the Scriptural view or claims of this:

Sins Effect and Decrees and the Slain Lamb.

Ephesians 1:4 *According as he hath chosen us in him before the foundation of the world, that we should be holy and without blame before him in love:*

Genesis 2:17 *But of the tree of the knowledge of good and evil, thou shalt not eat of it: for in the day that thou eatest thereof thou shalt surely die.*

Genesis 3:6-7 *And when the woman saw that the tree was good for food, and that it was pleasant to the eyes, and a tree to be desired to make one wise, she took of the fruit thereof, and did eat, and gave also unto her husband with her; and he did eat. And the eyes of them both were opened, and they knew that they were naked; and they sewed fig leaves together, and made themselves aprons.*

Romans 5:12 *Wherefore, as by one man sin entered into the world, and death by sin; and so death passed upon all men, for that all have sinned:*

Man was given a legal requirement to obey to not eat of the forbidden fruit. Adam, with Eve, did and passed the sentence of sin and death to all human offspring. That only required one act of disobedient, law breaking.

Romans 5:17-18 *For if by one man's offence death reigned by one; much more they which receive abundance of grace and of the gift of righteousness shall reign in life by one, Jesus Christ.) Therefore as by the offence of one judgment came upon all men to condemnation; even so by the righteousness of one the free gift came upon all men unto justification of life.*

God instituted the temporary substitutionary blood sacrifice as a picture of the permanent sacrifice to come. All those believing in God's provision of the law by faith would be saved. This had to be done annually for the nation and regularly by the individual. It has always been a matter of faith in God's provision for sin.

Habakkuk 2:4 *Behold, his soul which is lifted up is not upright in him: but the just shall live by his faith.*

John 1:3 *All things were made by him; and without him was not any thing made that was made.*

Revelation 1:8 *I am Alpha and Omega, the beginning and the ending, saith the Lord, which is, and which was, and which is to come, the Almighty.*

Revelation 5:12 *Saying with a loud voice, Worthy is the Lamb that was slain to receive power, and riches, and wisdom, and strength, and honour, and glory, and blessing.*

When Jesus Christ the Son of God came as the Lamb slain from the foundation of the world He would die once as man's one-time permanent solution to sin. Salvation would be granted to all who truly believe in Christ as the perfect permanent sacrifice, or atonement – once for our sins.

Hebrews 10:12 *But this man, after he had offered one sacrifice for sins for ever, sat down on the right hand of God;*

Hebrews 10:14 *For by one offering he hath perfected for ever them that are sanctified.*

Hebrews 10:17-18 *And their sins and iniquities will I remember no more. Now where remission of these is, there is no more offering for sin.*

Hebrews 9:28 *So Christ was once offered to bear the sins of many; and unto them that look for him shall he appear the second time without sin unto salvation.*

As a result, we need only once to ask for the permanent sacrifice to be applied to our soul. To need or require a person to regularly, or more than once, apply the perfect atoning sacrifice would mean we continually crucify Christ anew.

Hebrews 6:6 *If they shall fall away, to renew them again unto repentance; seeing they crucify to themselves the Son of God afresh, and put him to an open shame.*

It would mean God's legal requirement for sin was not truly satisfied by the one-time death of Christ. It would

11

mean also that Christ did not fulfill the Law as the last legal and permanent sacrifice for sin.

Matthew 5:17-18 *Think not that I am come to destroy the law, or the prophets: I am not come to destroy, but to fulfil. For verily I say unto you, Till heaven and earth pass, one jot or one tittle shall in no wise pass from the law, till all be fulfilled.*

It would mean that when the Savior cried out "It is finished" (a business term meaning the debt is paid in full or satisfied) it wasn't. Thus, we must "perform" some form of righteous law or works to keep ourselves assured and saved. So then, the object of our faith would be both in Christ's work and our own. But God, who decreed the law in Genesis 2 for man's test and obedience also provided for man's salvation when he would fall under sin. The temporary law was replaced by the permanent, Jesus Christ.

Hebrews 7:25 *Wherefore he is able also to save them to the uttermost that come unto God by him, seeing he ever liveth to make intercession for them.*

Hallelujah! We are saved and kept forever His because of our Lord's legal promise and provisions. He paid my debt so that salvation, permanent legal deliverance, is mine for the asking.

Have you asked yet?

If so, you're freed and "Forever His"!

Ephesians 1:4 *According as he hath chosen us in him before the foundation of the world, that we should be holy and without blame before him in love:*

The verse cited is a very exciting passage as is all of Ephesians 1. When considering this passage, we can see the flow of blessing. In verse 3 we are told that we have been blessed with all (everything and every type) spiritual blessings in heaven and in Christ. Our spiritual blessings are with and in Christ. In other words, we the believers were chosen to be in Christ as a part of our heavenly blessings. That is our standing or position.

Revelation 13:8 *And all that dwell upon the earth shall worship him, whose names are not written in the book of life of the Lamb slain from the foundation of the world.*

Revelation 21:27 *And there shall in no wise enter into it any thing that defileth, neither whatsoever worketh abomination, or maketh a lie: but they which are written in the Lamb's book of life.*

Furthermore, He did so from the beginning of the world (the foundation). That's incredible! God knew me personally as a believer before creation. He chose me as a New Testament believer to be in Christ and not Abraham or Israel. Why? So all believers in Him could be "Holy" (set apart and sainted), blameless, and before Him (a witness of) in love.

13

Ephesians 1 then discusses both our position and possessions in Christ in heavenly places. In verse 5, the believer was predestinated (predetermined, ordained, appointed) for something, not to something (like salvation). God has predetermined that the New Testament in Christ believers will be adopted. It's a done deal in God's mind. Furthermore, the word predestine also has with it the idea of fixing our boundaries so we can't go outside them. So that the thing predetermined will be because it pleases God. Why? He said so!

In verse 6, we have been graced or blessed, "made", accepted. Accepted – "kareeto" like "made" is graced. Literally we are graced into the already graced and in the well-loved. This too is a finished deal with God, and we are experiencing it the moment we get saved. It never stops!

In verse 7, the believer has redemption (payment of ransom, complete deliverance) by the blood payment of Christ. Furthermore, in Christ, the believer has forgiveness of sins. Forgiveness means to be liberated from bondage, the bondage or slavery of sin. This sin means our transgressions, whether knowingly or unknowingly. It's also applied to ALL sins, past, present, and future. Christ's ransom payment released us from sin forever. He made the provision, and the believer experiences a permanent effect.

Finally, in verse 7, the believer has also been predestined for God's own purposes to an inheritance promised and waiting for the believer, which He has secured and is delivering us to it.

Romans 8:29 *For whom he did foreknow, he also did predestinate to be conformed to the image of his Son, that he might be the firstborn among many brethren.*

Romans 8:29 declares that the "in Christ" the believer is being continuously conformed to the image of Christ. That, too, is their predestination, which is both their possession and position in Christ.

To make this really a done deal our Lord gave believers His Holy Spirit to seal them.

Romans 8:13 *For if ye live after the flesh, ye shall die: but if ye through the Spirit do mortify the deeds of the body, ye shall live.*

Literally, God has sealed the believer or set His "mark on them" which secures or preserves us.

Ephesians 4:30 *And grieve not the holy Spirit of God, whereby ye are sealed unto the day of redemption.*

In Ephesians 4:30, the Holy Spirit seals the believer "unto the day of redemption." That is our full redemption, heaven and our glorified bodies. No person, not ourselves or Satan, can take my salvation away. It is sealed and fixed and determined by God that I am forever possessed of Him and "Forever His".

This is my permanent possession in Him.

In review, our position is as a New Testament believer in Christ as opposed to being in Noah, Abraham, or Israel. This was determined by God before creation and the fall as man's permanent solution to sin. As a result, we are awaiting our predetermined possession of adoption, an inheritance, conformity to Christ, and our full redemption.

Romans 5:18 *Therefore as by the offence of one judgment came upon all men to condemnation; even so by the righteousness of one the free gift came upon all men unto justification of life.*

Romans 5:21 *That as sin hath reigned unto death, even so might grace reign through righteousness unto eternal life by Jesus Christ our Lord.*

Ephesians 2:5 *Even when we were dead in sins, hath quickened us together with Christ, (by grace ye are saved;)*

Ephesians 2:8-10 *For by grace are ye saved through faith; and that not of yourselves: it is the gift of God: Not of works, lest any man should boast. For we are his workmanship, created in Christ Jesus unto good works, which God hath before ordained that we should walk in them.*

Many years ago, during a personal tragedy, a pastor called me asking two questions. "Brother, is Christ enough? Is grace enough?" My broken-hearted response was short and simple. "Christ and His grace are all… all that is left…all that is sustaining us."

Without God's grace as the means of drawing us to Him, and providing a permanent solution to the sin problem, we would be left in part or in whole to do our own works. That of course is an impossible and unworkable situation.

Why is that? First, we are born with a sin nature. Sin left all humans sinners by decree in the garden, by genetic inheritance and by personal choice. No amount of moral, righteous behavior can undo our condition. We need a totally new nature, birth, and condition to save us. Man's condition is hopeless and absolutely depraved. Nothing man, in his actions, does before or after salvation contributes to his salvation. Salvation is all of grace or none at all. I am, by nature, as Paul says in Romans 7 both "exceedingly, thoroughly sinful and even sold (enslaved) under sin."

Romans 3:20 *Therefore by the deeds of the law there shall no flesh be justified in his sight: for by the law is the knowledge of sin.*

Romans 3:23 *For all have sinned, and come short of the glory of God;*

Romans 7:13 *Was then that which is good made death unto me? God forbid. But sin, that it might appear sin, working death in me by that which is good; that sin by the commandment might become exceeding sinful.*

Romans 7:14 *For we know that the law is spiritual: but I am carnal, sold under sin.*

Romans 7:18 *For I know that in me (that is, in my flesh,) dwelleth no good thing: for to will is present with me; but how to perform that which is good I find not.*

Ephesians 2:1-2 *And you hath he quickened, who were dead in trespasses and sins; Wherein in time past ye walked according to the course of this world, according to the prince of the power of the air, the spirit that now worketh in the children of disobedience:*

According to Ephesians 2:1-2, we were dead spiritually in sin and under the power of the devil ("the prince of the power of the air"). That is why Paul's discussion in Romans 7 is about why the practice of a moral law code, or the moral human will, is based on our old sin nature and always fails to save me, keep me saved or serve God. That leaves room for only being saved and secured forever as His, by grace.

So then, what is God's grace and how does it work? Grace is God's free gift of mercy to all who ask for it. It is unprompted by human effort, before or after salvation, or else it would not be free. It is therefore unmerited or unearnable. It is also unrepayable after the fact. Finally, it is underserved by anyone. We all deserve hell! It is God's grace that foresaw the human condition before creation and provided His grace program as our escape. That is why He is "*... rich unto all that call upon him.*" Romans 10:12.

Grace is much more than the means of completed and secured salvation. It is His means of enabling power to get saved and do His will. In grace He left me with my old sin (fleshly) nature to yield to, or my new nature in Christ to yield to.

Romans 7:14 *For we know that the law is spiritual: but I am carnal, sold under sin.*

To make it possible, He has given the believer His indwelling Holy Spirit to empower them and enable them to do His good will. This too is a part of His grace provision.

Romans 8:2 *For the law of the Spirit of life in Christ Jesus hath made me free from the law of sin and death.*

Therefore "His grace hath planned it all!" This is what Paul meant in Ephesians 2:8 *For by grace are ye saved through faith;…*" The means of being saved is GRACE. Being Saved is an event or action that begins at a definite time and never ends. Faith is the reason or cause which grace is supplied by Christ according to Galatians 2:20.

Galatians 2:20 *I am crucified with Christ: nevertheless I live; yet not I, but Christ liveth in me: and the life which I now live in the flesh I live by the faith of the Son of God, who loved me, and gave himself for me.*

Therefore, it can never be the result of any human effort at any time. Anything more would allow for minutest human pride, and input, or partnership.

Ephesians 2:9 *Not of works, lest any man should boast.*

Finally, the apostle Paul puts any works to rest by reminding us of our position, purpose and practice.

Ephesians 2:10 *For we are his workmanship, created in Christ Jesus unto good works, which God hath before ordained that we should walk in them.*

He has and is making us and not we ourselves. He has formed or manufactured (created) us in Christ Jesus for one purpose, good (godly) works. Like verse 9 states, salvation is not by human effort or enterprise (works). So, verse 10 states the good works we are to do are the by-product of God's effort which He has made ready or determined beforehand (ordained). This too is not subject to human opinion and religious rules.

But wait! Some might insist, what about James? Doesn't He say and illustrate in James 2:26, that "...faith without works is also dead."

The answer is a simple, yes. That statement, however, doesn't contradict Paul's statement that salvation is the result of "grace through faith" and "not of works". Remember, Ephesians 2:10 states that God created us (designed us, our salvation) unto "good works". James 2 and Ephesians 2:8-10 are saying the same thing to two separate audiences. The Ephesians Church was mainly Gentile. James' audience was exclusively Jewish trying to overcome the Law as salvation.

Both Paul and James agree that a true convert to Christ will pursue and prove God is (Christ's) righteousness. A false believer or apostate professes salvation, but their works betray them. It is they who will hear our Lord say, *"... I never knew you: depart from me, ye that work iniquity."* Matthew 7:23.

That is why ONLY God's grace saves you, keeps you, and keeps working in and through you by His grace provisions. Provisions such as the Holy Spirit, so we could walk in His righteousness. How absolutely humbling! And why? So we could be to the *"praise of*

His glory" Ephesians 1:12. So we would be "Forever His"!

The following verses are a few of the many passages which our Lord has left as His precious promises. Meditate upon them and comfort yourself with them, especially when discouraged or when the Tempter comes. Know that you are loved with an everlasting love and are Forever His.

John 3:16 *For God so loved the world, that he gave his only begotten Son, that <u>whosoever believeth</u> in him should not perish, but have <u>everlasting life</u>.*

John 3:18 *He that <u>believeth</u> on him is <u>not condemned</u>: but he that believeth not is condemned already, because he hath not believed in the name of the only begotten Son of God.*

John 3:36 *He that <u>believeth</u> on the Son <u>hath everlasting life</u>: and he that believeth not the Son shall not see life; but the wrath of God abideth on him.*

John 6:37 *All that the Father giveth me shall come to me; and him that cometh to me I will in <u>no wise cast out</u>.*

John 6:40 *And this is the will of him that sent me, that every one which seeth the Son, and <u>believeth on him</u>, may have <u>everlasting life</u>: and I will raise him up at the last day.*

John 6:44 *No man can come to me, except the Father which hath sent me draw him: and I will raise him up at the last day.*

John 10:27-28 *My sheep hear my voice, and I know them, and they follow me: And I give unto them eternal life; and they shall never perish, neither shall any man pluck them out of my hand.*

Acts 13:48 *And when the Gentiles heard this, they were glad, and glorified the word of the Lord: and as many as were ordained to eternal life believed.*

Romans 5:1-2 *Therefore being justified by faith, we have peace with God through our Lord Jesus Christ: By whom also we have access by faith into this grace wherein we stand, and rejoice in hope of the glory of God.*

Romans 8:10 *And if Christ be in you, the body is dead because of sin; but the Spirit is life because of righteousness.*

Romans 8:14 *For as many as are led by the Spirit of God, they are the sons of God.*

Romans 8:35-39 *Who shall separate us from the love of Christ? shall tribulation, or distress, or persecution, or famine, or nakedness, or peril, or sword? As it is written, For thy sake we are killed all the day long; we are accounted as sheep for the slaughter. Nay, in all these things we are more than conquerors through him that loved us. For I am persuaded, that neither death, nor life, nor angels, nor principalities, nor powers, nor things present, nor things to come, Nor height, nor depth, nor* *any other creature, <u>shall be able to separate us</u> from the love of God, which is in Christ Jesus our Lord.*

Romans 10:*13 For <u>whosoever shall call</u> upon the name of the Lord <u>shall be saved.</u>*

Galatians 3:22 *But the scripture hath concluded all under sin, that the promise by faith of Jesus Christ might be <u>given to them that believe.</u>*

Philippians 2:13 *For it is God which worketh in you both to will and to do of his good pleasure.*

Colossians 2:10 *And <u>ye are complete in him,</u> which is the head of all principality and power:*

Colossians 3:4 *When Christ, who is our life, shall appear, then shall ye also appear with him in glory.*

Titus 3:5-7 *Not by works of righteousness which we have done, but according to <u>his mercy he saved us,</u> by the washing of regeneration, and renewing of the Holy Ghost; Which he shed on us abundantly through Jesus Christ our Saviour; That <u>being justified by his grace,</u> we should be made heirs according to the hope of eternal life.*

Hebrews 13:5 *Let your conversation be without covetousness; and be content with such things as ye have: for he hath said, <u>I will never leave thee, nor forsake thee</u>.*

1 John 5:13 *These things have I written unto you that believe on the name of the Son of God; that ye may know that <u>ye have eternal life,</u> and that ye may believe on the name of the Son of God.*

Revelation 2:7 *He that hath an ear, let him hear what the Spirit saith unto the churches; To him that overcometh will I give to eat of the tree of life, which is in the midst of the paradise of God.*

Revelation 2:11 *He that hath an ear, let him hear what the Spirit saith unto the churches; He that overcometh shall not be hurt of the second death.*

Revelation 3:5 *He that overcometh, the same shall be clothed in white raiment; and I will not blot out his name out of the book of life, but I will confess his name before my Father, and before his angels.*

Dr. Tobin has written several other books & booklets. They can be found on his church website: www.TomahBaptistChurch.com.

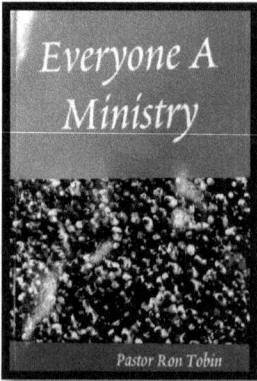

Everyone a Ministry

Dr. Tobin describes how the local church already has all the people and gifts it needs to do the work God has given. Follow the journey and detailed format of a church and their pastor to change their idea of ministry forever. This will be an invaluable resource for any church who wants to see how everyone can become a ministry for Christ in their daily life.

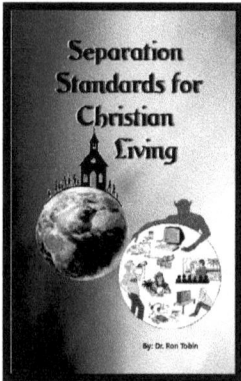

Separation Standards for Christian Living

This book makes an excellent personal or family devotional. It is also greatly used for a large or small group Bible study. Both student or teacher will not be disappointed by the information presented by these, once widely held convictions and standards of Bible believers.

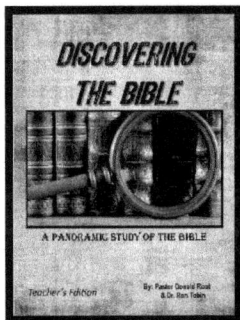

Discovering the Bible
(Teacher & Student's Editions)

Co-Authored with Pastor Don Root, this 10-lesson study takes a student through the entire Bible with a "fly over the forest" approach rather than an "inspect the bark on the trees" approach. It introduces the key characters, events, and themes of Scripture from a dispensational perspective. The student's edition utilizes fill-in-the-blank, matching, and multiple choice questions to draw the user into an interactive study. Filled with charts, maps, and timelines, the study also weaves in events from secular history to demonstrate that events in Scripture happened in the same world. The teacher's edition contains all the correct answers as well as teaching commentary. This makes it an excellent choice for individual discipleship or for the whole church.

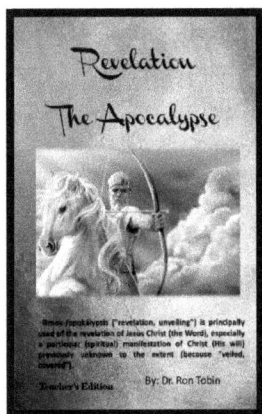

Revelation: The Apocalypse

This series is a wonderful Sunday School or Institute study of the book of Revelation. This has both a separate teachers and student edition. The student edition has blanks to fill in that correspond with the answers given in the teacher's edition. Each page and chapter is filled with amazing color pictures. These pictures can be purchased separately as a PowerPoint presentation that coordinates with the book chapters.

Principle Lessons for the New Pastor This is short, but an excellent guide for a new or young pastor, or college student in the early stages of their pastorate. The principles are seldom taught in seminary but confront a pastor early in his ministry. The booklet will make an excellent companion to devotions.

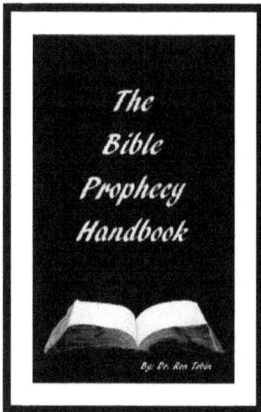

The Bible Prophecy Handbook

– This book originated as a Bible Institute course. Later it developed as an adult Bible class and sermon series. The reader will gain invaluable insights into understanding Bible prophecy, past, and future, without wading in too deep of water. It, of course, approaches the subject from a dispensational, pre-millennial, and pre-tribulation position.

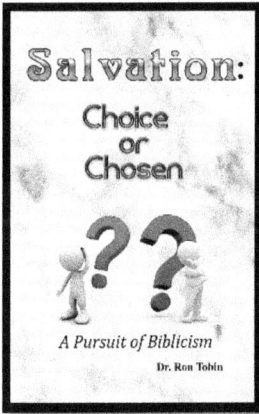

Salvation: Choice or Chosen-

This book is a timely, concise study of the subject of man's salvation. It attempts to answer the question does man have a viable choice in salvation or is it fixed? This balanced work attempts to show some of the errors, origin, and philosophies of Calvinism. With Calvinism's modern resurgence, the book serves as a warning to all who yearn for Revival and Bible Evangelism. The book is a clarion call to seek or return to being true Biblicist. May we be faithful like the Bereanites until the Lord returns. Maranatha!

ABOUT THE AUTHOR

Dr. Tobin has served the Lord for over forty years as a Pastor, as well as an educator in college and high school. His passion is the pastorate where he has been involved in church planting of three works and pastoring existing works. It was as a young elementary student that God began to move in his heart to become a missionary and pastor, even while in a Catholic parochial school.

While under Catholic training (Jesuits, Carmelites, and Augustinians), Dr. Tobin initially began to adopt the Augustinian Theology. However, in the turbulent 1960's he turned briefly in the exact opposite direction rejecting God's rules or religion. Instead, Pastor Tobin turned to Marxism, and through that emptiness, he turned to mysticism.

Gloriously he came to know Jesus Christ in the fall of 1971. Since then, his pursuit has been Christ. It was not difficult to fall back upon Augustinian Theology, now considered Calvinism. After many years of study, however, Dr. Tobin was convinced biblically and practically of the extremes or errors of Calvinism. This is especially true today of the New Covenant (Calvinist) Movement.

Dr. Tobin holds undergraduate degrees in the Bible and several secular studies. He also holds an earned MTH and Doctrine of Ministry.

www.ingramcontent.com/pod-product-compliance
Lightning Source LLC
Chambersburg PA
CBHW071753020426
42331CB00008B/2300